the great sushi and sashimi cookbook

whitecap

This edition published in 2004 in the US and Canada by Whitecap Books Ltd.

For more information, contact Whitecap Books,

351 Lynn Avenue, North Vancouver, British Columbia, Canada V7J 2C4

Project Manager: Anthony Carroll

Food Photography: Warren Webb

Sushi Chefs: Masakazu Hori and Kazu Takahashi

Food Stylists: Kazu Takahashi and Masakazu Hori

Recipe Development of North American edition: Kazu Takahashi and Masakazu Hori

Creative Director: Paul Sims

Design: Paul Sims

Proofreader: Andrea Tarttelin

Editor of North American edition: Marial Shea

The publishers would like to thank Mr. Kazu Takahashi and his staff of the Sushi Bar Rashai, authentic Japanese Restaurant at

241 Parramatta Road, Annandale NSW, for his help and assistance in the compilation of this book.

National Library of Canada Cataloguing in Publication Data

Main entry under title:

The great sushi and sashimi cookbook / editor, Marial Shea; sushi chefs, Masakazu Hori and Kazu Takahashi. North American edition.

(Great seafood series)

Includes index.

ISBN 1-55285-542-2

1. Sushi. 2. Cookery, Japanese. 3. Cookery (Seafood) I. Hori, Masakazu, 1970- II. Takahashi, Kazu, 1954- III. Shea,

Marial. IV. Series.

TX724.5.J3G74 2003   641.5952   C2003-911226-8

Computer typeset in: Humanist, Skia and Garamond Italic

Printed in Indonesia

The publisher acknowledges the financial support of the Government of Canada through the Book Publishing
Industry Development Program for our publishing activites.

Contents

Introduction

It's a mystery. How can something so simple seem so incredibly complicated?

If you're new to sushi, it's no wonder you're a little intimidated. There's the language, the customs . . . and what a dazzling array of ways to eat fish! Rice cubes topped with all manner of sea delicacies . . . bite-sized rolls . . . little seaweed "boats" . . . artfully arranged slices of raw fish.

Your friends, of course, are no help at all. Half swear they hate the stuff, particularly those who haven't tried it, and the ones who love it are too enthused over the anago (sea eel) or raving about uni (sea urchin — see glossary on page 118) to help a novice make a less exotic selection. Help is at hand — read on!

Then and Now

Japan is an island nation, its surrounding seas warmed by Kuroshio, the plankton-rich Japan Current, and abundant with an astonishing variety of fish and shellfish. The islands themselves are mountainous, and what little arable land exists is terraced and carefully cultivated to coax rice and a few other crops. Japan has always fed its dense population from the sea and the rice fields, its cuisine emphasizing what nature provides. Sushi, the combination of raw fish and seasoned rice that seems so exotic to foreigners, is a supremely logical food in Japan.

Sushi began centuries ago in Japan as a method of preserving fish. It is told that the origins of sushi came from countries of Southeastern Asia. Cleaned, raw fish were pressed between layers of rice and salt and weighted with a stone. After a few weeks, the stone was removed and replaced with a light cover, and a few months after that, the fermented fish and rice were considered ready to eat. Some restaurants in Tokyo still serve this original style of sushi made with freshwater carp called narezushi. Its flavor is so strong that it obscures the identity of the fish altogether, making narezushi something of an acquired taste.

It wasn't until the eighteenth century that a clever chef named Yohei decided to forgo the fermentation and serve sushi in something resembling its present form. It became very popular and two distinct styles emerged: Kansai style, from the city of Osaka in the Kansai region, and Edo style, from Tokyo, which was then called Edo. Osaka has always been the commercial capital of Japan, and the rice merchants there developed sushi that consisted primarily of seasoned rice mixed with other ingredients and formed into decorative, edible packages. Tokyo, located on a bay then rich with fish and shellfish, produced nigiri-sushi, featuring a select bit of seafood on a small pad of seasoned rice. Although the ornamental sushi of the Kansai region is still very popular, it is nigiri-sushi that foreigners are most familiar with.

The Art of Sashimi

Within minutes of picking up the menu in a sushi restaurant, you'll realize that the ideal way of cooking fish may well be not cooking it at all! The heart and soul of sashimi is the freshest fish served raw, chilled, skilfully sliced and artfully arranged. Since sashimi is raw fish on its own, without rice, only the finest cuts are used.

The biggest hurdle — when you come "face to fin" with your first sushi experience — is knowing what you're getting into. Not to worry. All you need is a few more facts and a little less attitude. Just a couple of tips about how to navigate these new waters. By reading this book you will not only learn how to make sushi and sashimi, you will get some insight into the whole sushi experience.

Equipment

This is a basic set of utensils for making sushi.

Rice-cooling tub (hangiri)

Used for cooling the vinegared rice giving it the perfect texture and gloss. It is made of cypress bound with copper hoops, but any wooden or plastic vessel can be used instead.

Spatula (shamoji)

Used to turn and spread sushi rice while cooling it. Traditionally the spatula is a symbol of the housewife's position in the household. You can use an ordinary spoon instead, wooden or plastic.

Fan (uchiwa)

Used to drive off moisture to get the right texture and flavor of sushi rice. Originally this fan was made of bamboo ribs covered with either paper or silk. If no fan is available, a piece of cardboard or a magazine can be used instead.

Bowl

A large bowl with a lid is necessary to keep the cooked sushi rice warm while making your sushi.

Chopping board (manaita)

This is a must. Traditionally made of wood, but nowadays many people prefer chopping boards made of rubber or resin, as these are easier to keep clean.

Chopsticks (saibashi)

There are two types of chopsticks: long chopsticks for cooking, often made from metal, and shorter chopsticks for eating.

Tweezers

Used to remove small bones from fish. Larger, straight-ended tweezers are better than the smaller variety commonly found in the bathroom and can be obtained from fish markets or specialty stores.

Rolling mat (makisu)

Made of bamboo woven together with cotton string, this is used to make rolled sushi.

Knives

The only way to get nicely cut surfaces is to use steel knives of good quality. Use whetstones to sharpen the blades yourself. Good Japanese knives are an outgrowth of forging the Japanese sword which is world famous for its sharpness. The knives are a chef's most valuable possessions and sushi chefs keep a wet cloth nearby, frequently wiping the blades to keep their knives clean as they work. Here are the basic types:

Cleavers (deba-bocho).

Wide heavy knives with triangular-shaped blades capable of cutting bone.

Vegetable knives (nakiri-bocho).

Lighter than cleavers, these have rectangular blades.

Fish knives (sashimi-bocho).

Long and slender, with the pointed type being most popular in Osaka and the blunt-ended type most popular in Tokyo. Excellent for filleting and slicing fish, they are also just right for slicing rolled sushi.

7

Ingredients

Vinegar

Sugared water or any alcoholic beverage, allowed to stand long enough, naturally sours and becomes vinegar. The word in itself is French and comes from *vin* (wine) and *aigre* (sour). In Japan it is made from rice, the grain from which sake is brewed. With the power to alter proteins, vinegar destroys bacteria. Adding sugar
to sushi rice is to prevent the tartness of vinegar from coming through too strongly.

Soy Sauce

Soy sauce is popular all over the world, used under many appellations: all flavor, meat sauce, all-purpose seasoning, etc.

Japanese soy sauce, rather than the darker and richer Chinese variety, is the one for sushi lovers. Soy sauce is highly recommended as a natural fermented
food, superior to salt, sugar or synthetic seasonings. It is essential to most traditional Japanese foods, including sushi, tempura, sukiyaki and noodles.

To tell good soy sauce from bad, use the following guidelines:

Aroma. A good soy sauce never produces an unpleasant smell, no matter how deeply you inhale.

Color. When a small quantity is poured into a white dish, good soy sauce looks reddish.

Clarity. Good soy sauce is perfectly translucent. Sunlight passing through it gives it a lovely glow.

Once opened, soy sauce should be stored in a cool, dark, dry place or refrigerated.

Pickled Ginger (gari or shoga)

Ginger is used to cleanse the palate between bites of sushi. It does not take a lot of ginger to cleanse the palate, so that a small pile should be enough for several rolls. Pickled ginger can be bought in Asian food stores, but if you wish to make your own, try this recipe.

ingredients:

8oz/250g fresh ginger

⅓ cup/90mL rice vinegar

2 tablespoons/25mL mirin

2 tablespoons/25mL sake

5 teaspoons/25mL sugar

Instructions

1 Scrub the ginger under running water. Blanch in boiling water for one minute, drain and cut into medium-sized pieces.

2 Combine rice vinegar, mirin, sake and sugar in a small pan. Bring to a boil, stirring until the sugar has dissolved. Cool.

3 Place the ginger in a sterilized jar and pour the cooled vinegar over it. Cover and keep 3–4 days before using. Will keep refrigerated for up to one month.

4 Although the pale pink color develops as it ages, you might want to add a small amount of red food coloring.

5 Slice thinly before serving.

Nori (seaweed)

After harvesting, this seaweed is dried, toasted and sold packaged in standard size sheets (7$\frac{1}{2}$x8$\frac{1}{2}$in/19x21cm). Once the sealed cellophane or plastic bag has been opened, nori should be eaten at once or stored in a sealed container in a dry, cool, dark place to preserve its crispiness. Nori is particularly rich in vitamins A, B$_{12}$ and D. Nori belts are used on nigiri-sushi when the topping being used is likely to slip off the rice, such as omelet and tofu (see page 92).

Tezu

A bowl of half sushi vinegar and half water, used to wet hands, knife, seal nori rolls, etc., making it easier to handle sushi rice and toppings.

Sake

A colorless brewed alcoholic beverage made from rice, legally defined as a rice beer. Its bouquet is somewhat earthy, with subtle undertones; it has a slightly sweet initial taste, followed by a dry aftertaste. Sake should be stored in a cool, dark place prior to opening, then in the refrigerator after opening. Very popular in Japan, it is the traditional drink served before eating sushi, and should be served warm.

Mirin

Mirin is know as sweet sake, and is generally only used for seasoning. If unavailable, sweet sherry makes a suitable substitute.

Daikon radish

A Japanese white radish, available fresh in Asian stores, in sizes ranging from 6in/15cm to 3ft/90cm. It may be refrigerated for several weeks. Cut into very fine slivers, it is commonly eaten with sashimi and can be used as a substitute for nori seaweed. When it is minced, it can be added to soy sauce for different texture and flavor.

Tofu

Custard-like cake of soybean curd, about 3in/8cm square. Sold fresh in supermarkets, it will keep for several days if refrigerated submerged in fresh water. Tofu is used in nigiri-sushi as a substitute for sushi rice, or as a topping on the rice.

Sushi Rice

When it comes to sushi, the rice is as important as the fish, and it takes years of training to learn how to make perfect sushi rice. There are different ways of doing it, but by following the directions on page 80 you will have a universally accepted and uncomplicated method of making the rice.

Sesame seeds

White sesame seeds are roasted and used as an aromatic seasoning, while black seeds are mostly used as a garnish.

Wasabi

Grown only in Japan, wasabi horseradish, when grated finely, is a pungent, refreshing pulp that removes unpleasant fishiness. Fresh wasabi is very expensive and difficult to obtain, so the best alternative is the powdered variety. Mix it with water to get a firm consistency. The wasabi purchased in tubes tends to be too strong and lacks that real wasabi flavor.

Mayonnaise

Not extensively used in sushi cooking, with the notable exception of the California roll.

Instead of using the standard commercially-made egg mayonnaise, try this homemade variety with a slight Japanese influence.

ingredients:

3 egg yolks

½ teaspoon/2mL lemon juice

¼ cup/50mL white miso

1 cup/250mL/8fl oz vegetable oil

salt to taste

sprinkle of white pepper

a pinch of grated yuzu, lime, or lemon peel

Instructions

1 In a bowl, beat the egg yolks and lemon juice with a wooden
spoon.

2 Continue to beat, adding the vegetable oil a few drops
at a time until the mixture begins to emulsify. Keep on
adding the rest of the oil.

3 Stir in the miso and the seasonings.

4 Refrigerate before using.

Note: Yuzu is a Japanese orange used
only for its rind. Kaffir lime used in Thai
or Malaysian food is an alternative, as is
lemon or lime rind.

Flat cut

Sashimi Cuts

There are 5 basic fish-cutting methods for sashimi and sushi, and a very sharp, heavy knife is indispensable to them all.

Flat cut (hira giri)

This is the most popular shape, suitable for any filleted fish. Holding the fish firmly, cut straight down in slices about $^1/_4$ -$^1/_2$in/$^1/_2$-1cm and 2in/5cm wide, depending on the size of the fillet.

Thread shape (ito zukeri)

Although this technique may be used with any small fish, it is especially suitable for squid. Cut the squid straight down into $^1/_4$in/$^1/_2$cm slices, then cut lengthwise into $^1/_4$in/$^1/_2$cm-wide strips.

Cubic cut (kazu giri)

This style of cutting is more often used for tuna. Cut the tuna as for the flat cut, then cut into $^1/_2$in/1cm cubes.

Paper-thin slices (usu zukuri)

Place any white fish fillet, such as sole or snapper, on a flat surface and, holding quite firmly with one hand, slice it at an angle into almost transparent sheets.

Angled cut (sori giri)

The ideal cut for sushi topping. Starting with a rectangular piece of fish, such as salmon or tuna, cut a trianglar piece from one corner, and continue slicing off pieces approximately $^1/_4$-$^1/_2$in/$^1/_2$-1cm thick.

Angled cut

How to Eat Sushi

A lot of Japanese do not know the correct ways to eat sushi. Eating it as explained below will maximize the flavors and experience of this great food. Here are the 2 ways to eat your sushi:

Method 1

1 Turn the sushi on its side and pick up both the side topping and the rice with chopsticks or thumb, index and middle fingers.
2 Dip the end of the topping, not the rice, in soy sauce.
3 Put the sushi into your mouth with the topping side directly on your tongue.

Method 2

1 Pick up some pickled ginger and dip it into the soy sauce.
2 Apply soy sauce over the topping, using the ginger as a brush.
3 Put the sushi into your mouth with the topping side directly on your tongue.

There is no set order in which the various kinds of sushi are eaten, except that the nori-wrapped pieces should be eaten first, since the crispness of nori seaweed does not last long once it comes in contact with the damp rice.

Don't soak it in too much soy sauce. The rice falls apart and the taste of soy will dominate. The same goes for wasabi and pickled ginger. Be very moderate, or else the taste of the topping and the rice will be concealed instead of complemented.

In modern sushi shops you may be served any drink you like with your sushi, but sake and green tea are always obligatory. Sake is served warm, before you eat — not during the meal and not after. The tea on the other hand is served during the whole meal. Green tea is essential for the full enjoyment of sushi as it removes aftertastes and leaves the mouth fresh for the next serving.

Health and Sushi

Sushi is praised by nutritionists as a balanced and healthy food because it contains many nutrients, including some minerals and vitamins, that would be partially destroyed by cooking.

Rice

Rice is an excellent source of complex carbohydrates which provide energy that is slowly released. It is also a good source of B vitamins.

Fish and seafood

Most seafood is low in calories, even lower than the leanest chicken and meat. It is also an excellent source of top quality protein and minerals, including iodine, zinc, potassium and phosphorus. It is rich in vitamins, especially the B group. The small amount of fat in fish is rich in omega-3 fatty acids, making fish a great heart food. Omega-3 fatty acids from fish can stop blood clots forming and blocking off arteries, thus reducing the risk of heart attack.

Nori

Seaweed is an excellent source of iodine, calcium and iron, all important for maintaining healthy blood and bone structure. It is also remarkable for being high in vitamin B_{12}, normally only found in animal products.

Soybeans

The soybean provides the best quality protein of all legumes. It is used to make tofu, soy sauce and miso. While some soy products contain a high amount of fat, soybeans have been proven to lower cholesterol. They also provide dietary fiber, some B-group vitamins, a range of minerals and antioxidents.

Wasabi

This essential sushi condiment provides an excellent source of vitamin C.

Nigiri-Sushi ...

The word sushi alone usually refers to the hand shaped nigiri-sushi, commonly served at sushi restaurants. Nigiri-sushi originated in Tokyo (known as Edo prior to 1868), with many varieties using some type of seafood or fish. The reason for this might relate to the fact that the city was rich in seafood of all kinds. Nigiri-sushi means "pressed by the hand" and generally consists of a piece of cooked or raw fish pressed across a rectangular pad of rice. It is often served with wasabi and dipped in soy sauce just before eating.

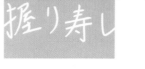

Making Nigiri-Sushi

Instructions

Most important when making nigiri-sushi is the balance between the topping and the rice. It is hand-formed by gently squeezing the ingredients together. You need a chopping-board, a sharp knife and a bowl of vinegared water (tezu) in which to rinse the fingers, the fish and the prepared rice. Remember, one of the most important criteria of well-made sushi is that the rice does not break when you pick it up.

1

Prepare the tezu, which consists of half water, half sushi vinegar. Moisten fingers and palms with the tezu. Most beginners put too much water on their hands. Use only a small amount.

2

Pick up a piece of fish in one hand, and with the other a small handfull of prepared sushi rice. Gently squeeze the rice to form a block. Most beginners hold too much rice. Take less than you think you need.

3

With the piece of fish laying in the palm of your hand, a small amount of wasabi can be spread along the fish.

4

With the piece of fish still in your palm, the rice can be placed on top of the fish. Use your thumb and press down slightly on the rice, making a small depression.

5

Using the forefinger from the other hand, press down on the rice, causing it to flatten.

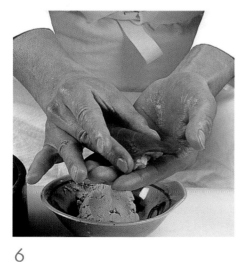

6

Turn the sushi over (fish side up) and, using the thumb and middle finger, squeeze the rice together.

7

Position fingers and hand as above, covering the fish and rice. Gently squeeze around the sushi. Repeat steps 5–7 twice more.

8

You should now have a piece of finished sushi, with the fish covering the firm rice.

Nigiri-Sushi with Prawns (Ebi)

Instructions

1 Insert a bamboo skewer through each prawn to prevent curling.

2 Drop the prawns into a saucepan holding 2 cups/500mL of boiling water and the salt and vinegar, and simmer for 2–3 minutes.

3 Scoop out prawns and drop them into ice water. Refresh with more cold water if necessary to ensure prawns are well chilled.

4 Twist skewers to remove prawns. Then shell prawns removing the legs and head but leaving the tips of the tails intact.

5 To remove the vein, slice lengthwise along the back and pull vein out.

6 Insert the knife along the leg side of the prawn and open like a butterfly.

7 Soak in salted water for 20 minutes. Then transfer into a bowl containing the vinegar water and soak for a further 20 minutes.

8 Proceed to make nigiri-sushi as described on pages 18–19.

ingredients:

10 thin bamboo skewers, 5in/15cm long
10 green king prawns
2 cups/500mL water
1 teaspoon/5mL salt
1 teaspoon/5mL vinegar

vinegar water:
2 cups/500mL water
1 cup/250mL vinegar

2 cups/500mL sushi rice (see page 80)
2 teaspoons/10mL wasabi

Makes 10 pieces

握り寿し

Nigiri-Sushi with Salmon
(Sake)

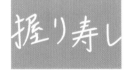

Instructions

1   Using the flat or angled cut (see page 13), slice the fillet thinly.

2   Proceed using the nigiri-sushi making techinique on page 18–19.

Makes 20 pieces

ingredients:
10oz/300g salmon fillet
2 cups/500mL sushi rice (see page 80)
1 tablespoon/15mL wasabi

Nigiri-Sushi with Tuna (Maguru)

Instructions

1   Slice the fillet using the flat or angled cut on page 13.

2   Proceed using the nigiri-sushi making techinique on page 18–19.

Note: Several different varieties of tuna are available at the fish market and to the fisherman. The 4 recommended types of tuna are:

Bluefin tuna — considered by most Japanese to be the superior fish in the tuna family.

Bigeye tuna — also highly regarded, exceeded in price on the Japanese markets only by the bluefin tuna.

Yellowfin tuna — an extremely important and widely resourced tropical tuna.

Albacore — well regarded for sashimi, but quite high in calories. Often refered to as "chicken of the sea" with its slight chicken flavor when cooked.

ingredients:

10oz/300g **tuna fillet**

2 cups/500mL **sushi rice (see page 80)**

1 tablespoon/15mL **wasabi**

Makes 20 pieces

Opposite: Salmon, prawn and tuna sushi

Nigiri-Sushi with Cockles (Torigai)

Instructions

ingredients:

6 cockles in the shell
½ cup/125mL sushi rice
(see page 80)
1 teaspoon/5mL wasabi

1 Soak cockles in fresh water for minimum 3 hours to discard any sand.

2 Open cockles as you would an oyster (page 98).

3 Proceed to make nigiri-sushi as described on pages 18–19.

Note: The cockle is a mollusk with two ridged oval shells hinged by a ligament near the pointed end. Cockles are always sold in the shell. Do not buy them if they're open. They have a rich sea taste.

Makes 6 pieces

Opposite: Cockle Sushi (left) and Seared Scallop

Sushi (right)

(Hotatagai) Nigiri-Sushi with Seared Scallops

ingredients:
6 scallops
½ cup/125mL sushi rice
(see page 80)
1 teaspoon/5mL wasabi

Makes 6 pieces

Instructions

1 Sear scallops (either roe on or off, personal preference) on very hot grillplate or fry for 20 seconds each side.

2 Proceed to make nigiri-sushi as described on pages 18–19.

Note: Scallops are available in both half-shell and meat form. Shelling the scallop is simply a matter of sliding a knife between the scallop and shell and lifting apart.

Nigiri-Sushi with Marinated Fish   (Zuke)

Instructions

1   Place the tuna fillet on a cutting board over a sink.
2   Cover tuna with a cloth then pour boiling water all over it.
3   Put in cold water immediately.
4   Mix mirin and sake.
5   Wipe tuna dry thoroughly, then put into the bowl with mixed sake and mirin.
6   Leave the tuna in marinade for about 2 or 3 hours.
7   Thinly slice the fillet (see page 13).
8   Make nigiri-sushi as described on pages 18–19.

ingredients:

100oz/300g **tuna (or bonito) fillet**
boiling water
bowl of cold water
½ cup/125mL/4fl oz **mirin**
½ cup/125mL/4fl oz **sake**
2 cups/500mL **sushi rice**
(see page 80)
1 tablespoon/15mL **wasabi**

Makes 20 pieces

Nigiri-Sushi with Grilled Salmon Belly   (Sake toro)

ingredients:

7oz/200g **salmon belly, skin on**
1 teaspoon/5mL **salt**
1 teaspoon/5mL **sake**
1⅓ cups/325mL **sushi rice**
   (see page 80)
1 tablespoon/15mL **grated white radish**

Instructions

1   Sprinkle salt and sake over the salmon's skin.
2   Grill on the skin side for about 2 minutes.
3   Remove from heat then leave until salmon cools.
4   Thinly slice salmon belly and prepare as for nigiri-sushi on pages 18–19.
6   Place white radish on top of sushi as a garnish.

Makes 15 pieces

Note: The salmon belly can be obtained from a fishmonger. Simply request it when he/she is next cutting up a salmon. The belly is a very tasty, if somewhat fatty, piece of the salmon.

Opposite: (L-R)Nigiri-Sushi with Marinated Tuna,

Nigiri-Sushi with Grill Salmon Belly, Nigiri-sushi with

Grilled Bonito (follow recipe as for Grilled Salmon Belly)

Nigiri-Sushi with Squid (Ika)

Instructions

ingredients:

10oz/300g squid

1½ cups/375mL sushi rice

(see page 80)

1 teaspoon/5mL wasabi

1   Prepare squid as shown on page 98.

2   Cut the squid in the thread shape (ito zukeri) as shown on page 13.

3   Proceed to make nigiri-sushi as described on pages 18–19.

Makes 15 pieces

Nigiri-Sushi with

Seasonal White Fish (Shiromi)

ingredients:

7oz/200g any white fleshed fish, such as snapper, halibut or whiting

1½ cups/325mL sushi rice (see page 80)

1 teaspoon/5mL wasabi

Makes 15 pieces

Instructions

1   Cut the fish fillet paper-thin (usu zukuri) as described on page 13.

2   Proceed as for nigiri-sushi making techniques on pages 18–19.

握り寿し

Opposite: (L-R) Nigiri-Sushi with Seasonal White Fish (snapper and whiting) and Nigiri-Sushi with Squid

Nigiri-Sushi with Sea Eel (Anago)

1   Bring water to the boil, place eel in and allow to cook for about 1 minute and then refresh in cold water.
2   Add the soy sauce and sugar to the boiling water.
3   Place the eel back into the boiling water, cook for 20 minutes then remove from the heat.
4   Allow to cool and then proceed to make nigiri-sushi as described on pages 18–19.
5   Wrap nigiri-sushi with nori belts by cutting strips of nori ½ in/1cm wide and wrapping them around the topping and rice.

ingredients:
2 cups/500mL water
8oz/250g sea water eel fillet
3 tablespoons/45mL soy sauce
3 tablespoons/45mL sugar
1²/₃ cups/400mL sushi rice (see page 80)
20 nori belts

Makes 15–20 pieces

Nigiri-Sushi with Freshwater Eel (Unagi)

ingredients:
½ cup/125mL/4fl oz soy sauce
1 cup/250mL/8fl oz mirin
2 tablespoons/25mL sugar
1 pre-cooked freshwater eel
2 cups/500mL sushi rice (see page 80)

Instructions

1   Combine soy sauce, mirin and sugar in a saucepan. Bring to the boil and reduce until half remains.
2   Thinly slice the eel and grill for 2 minutes, basting with the reduced soy sauce mixture.

Note: A fresh unagi eel is very hard to obtain, and even harder to prepare. Asian supermarkets or a good fishmonger should have supplies of prepared unagi eel.

Opposite: (L-R) Unagi Sushi and Anago Sushi

Makes 20 pieces

Nigiri-Sushi with
Octopus (Tako)

Instructions

1. Cut heads off the octopuses and turn inside out.

2. Sprinkle 2 tablespoons/25mL salt over the octopuses and rub into flesh. (This will remove the sliminess).

3. Have a large pot of boiling water at the ready, adding 2 tablespoons/25mL each of salt, sushi vinegar and the green tea. Boil the octopus for 8–10 minutes.

4. Remove octopuses from boiling water and add to a pot of cold water that has been mixed with 2 tablespoons/25mL of salt and 4 tablespoons/60mL of sushi vinegar. Allow to sit for 10 minutes.

5. Thinly slice the octopuses and proceed to make nigiri-sushi as described on pages 18–19.

6. Wrap sushi with nori belts (see step 5, page 31).

ingredients:

2 medium-sized octopuses
(approx 1 lb/500g each),
cleaned
6 tablespoons/75mL salt
boiling water
6 tablespoons/75mL sushi vinegar
2 tablespoons/25mL Japanese
green tea (Ocha)
2 cups/500mL sushi rice
(see page 80)
15–20 nori belts

Makes 15–20 pieces

Opposite: (L-R) Octopus Sushi and Cuttlefish Sushi

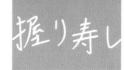

Nigiri-Sushi with
Leg of Cuttlefish
(Geso)

Instructions

ingredients:
1kg/2 lb **cuttlefish**
3 tablespoons/45mL **salt**
boiling water
2 tablespoons/25mL **sushi vinegar**
1 tablespoon/15mL **Japanese
green tea (Ocha)**
1½ cups/375mL **sushi rice
(see page 80)**
10–15 **nori belts**

1 Clean cuttlefish in the same manner as squid, as described on page 98.

2 Reserve the legs, using the hoods for tempura if desired.

3 Sprinkle 1 tablespoon/15mL salt over the cuttlefish and rub into flesh. (This will remove the sliminess).

4 Have a large pot of boiling water at the ready, adding 1 tablespoon/15mL each of salt, sushi vinegar and the green tea. Boil the cuttlefish for 8–10 minutes.

5 Remove cuttlefish from boiling water and add to a pot of cold water that has been mixed with 1 tablespoon/15mL each of salt and sushi vinegar. Allow to sit for 10 minutes.

6 Thinly slice the cuttlefish and proceed to make nigiri-sushi as described on pages 18–19.

7 Wrap sushi with nori belts (see step 5, page 31).

Makes 10–15 pieces

Nigiri-Sushi with Pickled
Yellowtail (BohSushi)

Instructions

1   Fillet the fish as directed on page 97.

2   Sprinkle salt all over fillets and let stand for
     15–20 minutes.

3   Rinse in fresh water.

4   Place in bowl and cover with rice vinegar, stand for
     25 minutes then remove to a colander to drain.

5   Proceed to make nigiri-sushi as described on page 80.

Makes 15 pieces

ingredients:

1 yellowtail (10-11oz/300-330g)

2 tablespoons/30mL salt

1 ¼ cups/300mL/10oz rice vinegar

1 ½ cups/375mL/7oz sushi rice (see page 80)

握り寿し

Chirashi Sushi

Instructions

The easiest type of sushi to make, made in all Japanese kitchens, is chirashi, or scattered, sushi. Chirashi-sushi is simply sushi rice with other ingredients mixed in or placed on the top. Chirashi-sushi without any seafood often makes its appearance in lunch boxes. It's taken on picnics and often sold on railway station platforms. Station lunches are not exclusively chirashi-sushi but many are. Stations are known for their type of food as well as for the unique containers in which they package their lunches. Again, the variations of this type of sushi are almost limitless. The rice can also be seasoned with a range of interesting ingredients such as chopped vegetables, sesame seeds, tofu pieces, chopped fresh and pickled ginger, crumbled nori and a variety of sauces.

suggestions for toppings:

tuna

prawns

omelet

cuttlefish

salmon

unagi eel

yellowtail

bonito

avocado

tofu

crab

vegetables

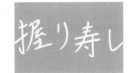

握り寿し

Tofu Sushi

1   Cut the tofu into nigiri-sized pieces.

2   Mix the ginger, shallot and soy sauce.

3   Prepare topping ingredients.

4   Place the topping onto the tofu and tie
    with nori belts (see page 31).

5   Put the mixed ginger on top then serve.

Note: The garnish already contains soy, so a bowl of soy and
wasabi is not necessary.

Makes 15–20 pieces

ingredients:
10oz/300g tofu (substitute
for sushi rice)
grated ginger
chopped shallot
1 teaspoon/5mL soy sauce
assortment of various fish,
meat and vegetables
15–20 nori belts

Opposite: Tofu Sushi, with (L-R) seared beef,

pickled yellowtail and smoked salmon

Maki-Sushi ...

Maki-sushi is a "rolled sushi". Maki means wrapping, and maki-sushi is narrow strips of different ingredients layered on a bed of vinegared rice all wrapped up with a sheet of nori or seaweed. Maki-sushi is the most well-known and varied sushi because just about any ingredient can be rolled into the center, from seafood to crisp vegetables, pickles, strips of omelet or avocado.

Cucumber Rolls (Kappamaki)

Instructions

1 Slice cucumber into strips.

2 Proceed to make cucumber rolls as described on page 82.

Note: You can further your variations by using ingredients such as fresh salmon, smoked salmon, prawns, avocado, minced tuna with chili, omelet and umeboshi plums instead of the cucumber.

Makes 24 pieces

ingredients:

4 pieces cucumber, each cut as
$\frac{1}{4}$ x $\frac{1}{2}$ x 3in/$\frac{1}{2}$ x 1 x 7$\frac{1}{2}$cm strips
2 sheets nori (cut in half)
1 cup/250mL sushi rice (see page 80)
1 teaspoon/5mL wasabi

Thin Sushi Rolls (Hosomaki)

Before making a sushi roll cut the nori in half, then cut the sheets so they have straight sides. The scraps can be used as nori belts.

Tuna Rolls (Tekkamaki)

ingredients:

2 nori sheets (cut in half)

1 cup/250mL sushi rice
(see page 80)

4 pieces tuna, each cut as
$\frac{1}{4}$ x $\frac{1}{2}$ x 3in/$\frac{1}{2}$ x 1 x 7$\frac{1}{2}$cm strips

1 teaspoon/5mL wasabi

Instructions

1 Slice tuna into strips.

2 Proceed to make tuna rolls as described on page 82.

Makes 24 pieces

巻き寿し

巻き寿し

Thick Rolls (Futomaki)

Instructions

1   Prepare the omelet, cucumber, avocado and eel by cutting into strips approximately
    $1/4 \times 1/2 \times 3$in / $1/2 \times 1 \times 7 1/2$cm long.

2   Proceed to make thick rolls as described on page 84.

Makes 16 pieces

ingredients:

3oz/75g omelet (see page 92)

1 cucumber

1 ripe avocado

3oz/75g pre-cooked eel fillet

2 nori sheets (cut in half)

1 tablespoon/15mL wasabi

3 cups/750mL sushi rice
(see page 80)

Dynamite Rolls (Spicy Tuna)

ingredients:

3oz/150g of tuna fillet, minced

1 teaspoon/5mL chili bean sauce
   (or Korean Kimchee to substitute)

2 green onions, chopped

2 nori sheets (cut in half)

1 tablespoon/15mL wasabi

3 cups/750mL sushi rice
   (see page 80)

Instructions

1   Combine tuna, chili bean sauce or Korean Kimchee and green
    onions.

2   Make rolls as described on page 84.

Makes 16 pieces

California Rolls

(Ura Makisushi)

Instructions

1. Shell and de-vein prawns, slice in half lengthwise. Slice avocado and cucumber.

2. Make California rolls as described on page 84.

Makes 24 pieces

Variations: Clean one large carrot, cut in thick strips and blanch. In salt water, blanch 30oz/90g English spinach, rinse in cold water, drain and shake dry. Cut 30oz/90g fresh salmon fillet in finger thick slices and marinate in mirin. Prepare the California roll as described.

ingredients:

4 medium cooked prawns or seafood sticks

1 ripe avocado, peeled, seeded and sliced

1 cucumber, cut into thin slices

8 teaspoons/40mL flying fish roe

4–8 leaf lettuce leaves

2 nori sheets (cut in half)

3 cups/750mL sushi rice (see page 80)

1 tablespoon/15mL wasabi

3 tablespoons/45mL Japanese mayonnaise (see page 10)

巻き寿し

Inside-Out Rolls (Sakamaki)

Instructions

1. Prepare the fillings for the rolls. Slice salmon, avocado and cucumber into suitable lengths.

2. Proceed to make your inside-out rolls as directed on page 86.

Note: Fillings can be varied depending on seasonal availability of ingredients. Avocado is not always available, so choose whatever suits your taste. Instead of flying fish roe on the outside of the roll, sesame seeds, salmon roe or dried bonito flakes make tasty alternatives.

Makes 24 pieces

ingredients:

7oz/210g **salmon fillet**

1 **ripe avocado**

1 **cucumber**

2 **nori sheets (cut in half)**

3 cups/750mL **sushi rice (see page 80)**

8 teaspoons/40mL **flying fish roe**

1 tablespoon/15mL **wasabi**

巻き寿し

Four-Sides Rolls

(Shikai maki)

Instructions

1 Place 1 sheet of nori on bamboo mat.

2 Spread one third of the sushi rice onto the nori.

3 Place another sheet of nori on top of first layer.

4 Spread another third of the sushi rice onto the nori.

5 Proceed to make sushi roll as described on page 84.

6 Cut the roll lengthwise into quarters.

7 Place final sheet of nori on bamboo mat and spread last of the rice.

8 Turn the nori over and place onto a cloth, as described in Sakamaki (page 86). Place 4 quarters of the previously cut roll alongside each other, place the omelet in the middle and proceed to roll.

9 Roll and form a square, press the grated egg onto the sides and then cut into four equal pieces.

Makes 4 pieces

ingredients:

1½ nori sheets (whole sheet cut in half)

1⅔ cups/400mL sushi rice (see page 80)

sushi omelet cut into a

½in/1½cm square

kimi oboro (grated hard-boiled egg yolk)

巻き寿し

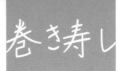

Temaki Sushi

ingredients:

5 nori sheets, halved

3 cups/750mL sushi rice
(see page 80)

wasabi

Temaki sushi originally was a meal for busy chefs. Having the ingredients on hand but no time to make sushi for themselves, they created this hand-roll sushi. Temaki offers a good way to experiment with ingredients such as cooked chicken, raw or rare beef and flavorsome sauces. They are quick and easy to prepare and taste delicious, even with an inexpensive filling. Small Temaki Sushi are perfect as an appetizer because they are easy to eat as finger food.

• If you cannot buy roasted nori sheets, you can roast them yourself. Lightly toast one side of the sheet of nori for about 30 seconds over a gas flame. Or toast them in a frying pan without oil on low heat until the aroma comes out. The nori will be crisp and have a dark green color after cooking. Leftovers from roasted nori sheets can be chopped and used as a seasoning or snack.

• If you make Temaki Sushi with soft or semi-liquid ingredients, it is easier with the rice at the bottom and the filling above it.

• Daikon radish sprouts are a popular ingredient for Temaki and Maki-Sushi and go well with omelet sushi. They resemble large mustard and cress, but are much hotter and spicier. Buy them in Asian supermarkets.

Suggestions for Fillings

tuna slices

spicy tuna (see page 44)

tempura prawns (see page 112)

teriyaki chicken

cooked prawns

crab sticks

unagi eel fillets

pickled whiting or yellowtail sashimi (see page 59)

flying fish, salmon or sea urchin roe

omelet

cucumber

avocado

smoked salmon (or any smoked fish)

instead of wasabi, try Japanese mayonnaise
   (page 10) or cream cheese

Follow instructions on pages 88–89.

Note: As an unusual variation or in case you run out of nori sheets, temaki sushi may even be rolled in lettuce, particularly cos (romaine) or iceberg. Lettuce makes a light, refreshing roll.

Makes 10 pieces

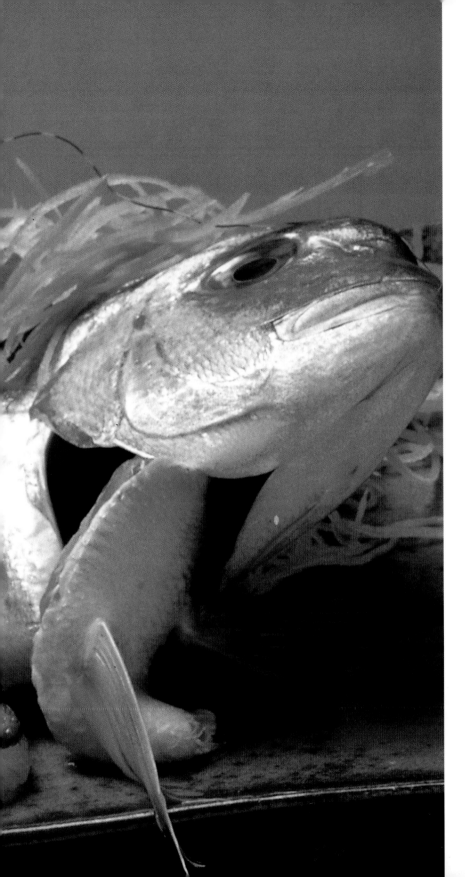

Sashimi...

The specialty of Japanese cuisine, sashimi is fresh fish served raw. The fish, which must be utterly fresh, is sliced paper thin or alternately one-quarter to one-half inch ($\frac{1}{2}$ - 1 cm) thick, cubed, or cut in strips, according to the nature of the fish. The sashimi is accompanied by wasabi and soy sauce. Sashimi is always part of a formal Japanese meal, served early while the palate is still clear in order for its nuances to be appreciated.

Garfish Sashimi

(Sayori)

Instructions

1 Clean, gut and fillet the garfish as described on
   page 97.
2 Cut the fillets into either the thread shape or
   paper-thin slices (see page 13).
3 Arrange on plate and sprinkle with shredded nori.

Note: The garfish has a fine, soft texture, a low to medium fat content
and a mild, sweet flavor. Care must be taken to remove all the bones.
garfish is also known as sea pike.

ingredients:
2 whole medium-sized garfish
shredded nori, for garnish

刺身

Pickled Whiting Sashimi
(Kisu)

ingredients:
2 fresh whole whiting
2 tablespoons/25mL salt
1 cup/250mL/8fl oz rice vinegar

Instructions

1 Clean, gut and fillet the whiting as described on page 97.

2 Sprinkle salt all over the fillets and allow to stand for 10–15 minutes

3 Rinse in fresh water.

4 Place fillets in a bowl and cover with the rice vinegar, allowing to stand for a further 10 minutes.

5 Remove from vinegar and drain in colander.

6 Cut the fillets into squares or paper-thin slices (see page 13).

Note: Whiting is a smaller member of the cod family.

Trevally Sashimi
(Shima-aji)

Instructions

1   Clean, gut and fillet the trevally as described on page 97.

2   Cut the fillets into a flat cut as directed on page 13.

3   Some paper-thin cuts may be cut and curled into a rose shape to make dish more attractive.

4   Serve garnished with shredded radish.

Note: The trevally is a member of the jack family and there are several varieties available. The smaller sizes make the better eating as the large fish tend to be somewhat drier and flavorless. Trevally has a firm, white flesh with a moderate fishy flavor and is an excellent , if somewhat underrated, fish for eating sashimi style.

ingredients:
1 whole trevally (approx 2lb/1kg)
shredded radish for garnish

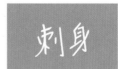

Tuna Sashimi

(Maguro)

Instructions

1 Proceed to cut tuna into flat cuts (see page 13).

2 To make Tosa Juya, put soy sauce, sake and dried bonito into a
   small saucepan and bring to the boil, stirring constantly, for
   2 minutes.

3 Strain through a fine sieve and cool to room temperature.
   Divide dipping sauce among small dishes and serve with
   tuna sashimi.

Note: If the fillet you have purchased has already been cut into a block,
you can proceed to cut the fish into the sashimi. If, on the other hand, the
fillet has not been trimmed and shaped into a block, then you may need to
buy a larger fillet and trim it down to size yourself, perhaps using the off-
cuts as minced tuna.

ingredients:

10oz/300g **sashimi-grade tuna fillet**

tosa juya (dipping sauce):
3 tablespoons/45mL **soy sauce**
2$\frac{1}{2}$ teaspoons/12mL **sake**
5 teaspoons/25mL **dried bonito (katsuobushi)**

Snapper Sashimi
(Tai)

Instructions

1   Clean, gut and fillet the snapper as described on page 97.

2   Flat cut the fillet or slice into paper-thin slices (see page 13).

3   Arrange the shredded carrot and endive on the plate as a garnish.

Note: While snapper is one of our most highly regarded cooking fish, it is also coming into its own as a sashimi fish, being served in many Japanese restaurants. It has a firm, white flesh with a sweet to mild flavor.

ingredients:
1 medium snapper (3 lb/1¹/₂kg)
shredded carrot
endive

刺身

Salmon Sashimi (Sake)

1 If purchasing a whole salmon, proceed to clean, gut and fillet the fish as described on page 97.

2 Trim away any dark or bruised flesh that may be evident, as well as any skin and fatty flesh.

3 Shape the fillets into a block and apply the flat cut (see page 13), cutting off required number of pieces. (Any off-cuts of salmon may be minced, mixed with wasabi and used in Battleship Sushi).

4 Arrange on plate and garnish with shredded daikon radish.

ingredients:

10oz/300g **sashimi-grade salmon or**
1 whole salmon
shredded daikon radish

刺身

Bonito Sashimi

(Katsuo)

Instructions

1   Clean, gut and fillet the bonito as described on page 97.

2   Flat cut the fillets (see page 13), leaving the skin on.

3   Arrange on serving plate, garnish with grated ginger.

Note: Bonito is a widely distributed fish, with varieties found around the world. The flesh is pink-red in color with a beautiful coarse grain and a rich flavor. If purchasing in fillet form, look for firm, moist flesh and marbling. The color is a good indicator of freshness. A freshly cut surface is very dull.

ingredients:

1 **whole bonito tuna (4lb/2kg)**
1 **teaspoon/5mL ginger, grated**

刺身

Yellowtail Sashimi
(Hamachi)

ingredients:
3 yellowtail
4 green onions, chopped
2 teaspoons/10mL ginger, grated

Instructions

1   Clean, gut and fillet the yellowtail as described on page 97.

2   Make sure all bones and skin are removed.

3   Cut the fillets thread shape (see page 13).

4   Combine the yellowtail, ginger and green onions together and sit
    for about 30 minutes, allowing the flavors to set.

Note: Yellowtail is a very popular fish in Japan for sashimi. The fillets tend
to be somewhat dry and oily, with a medium flavor. Some chefs suggest
cutting away the stronger tasting dark meat and using the milder, sweeter
light meat. You can save the dark scraps and add to the tuna in the
dynamite roll (see page 44).

刺身

Scampi Sashimi
(Tenagaebi)

Instructions

1. To prepare scampi, remove heads and set aside for garnish.

2. Peel back the underside shell from the top down to the tail.

3. Remove the flesh, discard the shells except bottom part of tail.

4. Place scampi meat on plate, putting head and tail on as garnish.

5. To make dipping sauce, warm sake in small saucepan then ignite it with a match, off the heat, and shake the pan gently until the flame dies out. Allow to cool. Put sake with the other ingredients and mix well. Pour into individual bowls and serve with scampi or any other sashimi.

Note: Scampi has a wonderfully sweet flesh, ideal for sashimi. It is considered by many to be even better than lobster. Hichimi togarashi (also known as shikimi togarachi) is a peppery Japanese condiment available at most Asian markets in hot, medium and mild.

ingredients:
8 scampi (if unavailable fresh, frozen is also good)

chirizu (spicy dipping sauce):
5 teaspoons/25mL sake
3 tablespoons/45mL freshly grated daikon radish
2 green onions, finely sliced
3 tablespoons/45mL soy sauce
3 tablespoons/45mL lemon juice
1/8 teaspoon/1/2 mL hichimi togarashi
(seven pepper spice)

Cuttlefish Sashimi
(Ika)

Instructions

1 Clean the cuttlefish or squid (see page 98).

2 To make cuttlefish and cucumber rolls, cut cuttlefish and nori into a sheet 2x4in/5x10cm.

3 Score the cuttlefish at $^1/_4$in/$^1/_2$cm intervals.

4 Place scored cuttlefish face down, lay nori on top, then cucumber and flying fish roe.

5 Roll up and cut into $^1/_2$in/1cm slices.

6 For cuttlefish and nori rolls, cut nori and cuttlefish into same size and place nori on top of cuttlefish.

7 Lightly score through the nori and into the cuttlefish and proceed to roll and cut into $^1/_2$in/1cm slices.

8 Cuttlefish can also be cut up into the thread shape cut (see page 13). Garnish with shredded nori.

Note: Cuttlefish is a mollusk and is generally smaller than a squid. They are highly prized in Japanese cuisine, with a flavor superior to that of the squid. When buying cuttlefish, look for firm flesh and undamaged bodies. Don't be put off by a broken ink sac, they are often broken when they are caught.

ingredients:
6 cuttlefish (or squid)
3 nori sheets
1 cucumber, cut into slices 4in/10cm long
1 teaspoon/5mL flying fish roe

Lobster Sashimi
(Ise Ebi)

Instructions

1   If lobster is purchased frozen, allow to defrost overnight in the refrigerator.

2   Remove the head and reserve for garnish.

3   Use poultry scissors to make a nice clean cut in the tail shell.

4   Pull the lobster meat out. Stuff the empty shell with shredded daikon radish for presentation. Cut the lobster into small sashimi slices.

5   Lay the meat on the daikon-stuffed tail, and serve.

Note: Traditionally, lobsters that were to be prepared as sashimi were purchased live and killed moments before being presented and served. The Japanese obsession with absolute freshness made this practice commonplace.

ingredients:
1 whole green (uncooked) lobster
endive
shredded carrot
shredded daikon radish

Techniques and Tips

All you need to know to assist you to become an accomplished home sushi chef.

Preparing Sushi Rice (Shari or Sushi Meshi)

Instructions

Rice cooked for sushi should be slightly harder in texture than for other dishes.
You will need approximately 1 cup/250mL of cooked rice for each roll. It is easier and
better to make too much rice than too little. Every recipe for sushi rice is different,
but they all work. You might find a recipe on the bottle of rice vinegar, on the bag
of rice, or on the package of nori.

Most recipes call for rinsing the raw rice until the water runs clear, but it can be avoided.
The reason it is rinsed first is to remove talc from the rice. Most rice seems to be coated
now with some sort of cereal starch, rather than talc, so rinsing could be omitted.
Tradition also suggests letting the rinsed rice drain in a colander, or zaru, for 30–60 minutes.
It's up to you. The rice you use should be short-grained rice.

1   Wash rice until water is clear (optional).

2   Combine the rice and water in a sauce pan and set aside for 30 minutes.

3   Bring rice and water to boil.

4   Reduce heat to very low and simmer for 10 minutes.

5   Turn off heat and leave for 20 minutes to steam.

6   Combine ingredients for sushi vineagar in a pan and heat, stirring, until dissolved.

7   Place the hot rice in a bowl and then sprinkle the sushi vinegar over the rice
     and mix it as if cutting. Use a fan to cool   until it reaches room temperature.

ingredients:

4 cups/1 litre short grain rice
4 cups/1 litre/35fl oz water

sushi vinegar:
½ cup/125mL/4fl oz rice vinegar
4 tablespoons/60mL sugar
2 teaspoons/10mL salt
1 teaspoon/5mL soy sauce

Preparing Sushi Rice

1

Rinse a Japanese wooden bowl (hangiri) or a flat wooden or plastic bowl with cold water before you place in the hot rice.

2

Add the sushi vinegar to the rice, pouring it over a paddle to help evenly dispense the vinegar.

3

Mix the vinegar into the rice, being careful not the flatten the rice.

4

Use a fan to help bring the rice back to room temperature.

Making Thin Sushi Rolls (Hosomaki)

1

Cut one nori sheet in half lengthwise and trim the sides so they're straight. Use two pieces for making the sushi rolls. Place nori shiny side down onto the mat.

2

Moisten your hands with some tezu and get a handful of rice from the rice-cooling tub. Spread the rice over the nori, taking care to do this evenly.

3

With your forefinger, spread the desired amount of wasabi across the rice, starting at one end and spreading it across the middle to the other end.

4

Place filling along the center of the rice, on top of the wasabi. Lift the edge of the bamboo mat.

5

With fingers from both hands hold onto the mat and the filling. Wrap the mat and nori over the filling, making sure all ingredients are evenly pressed.

6

Continue rolling, but applying a little more pressure to compact the rice. If needed, repeat the last step again to ensure the rice is pressed firmly and evenly along the roll.

7

Remove roll from the mat and place on a cutting board. Cut the roll in half.

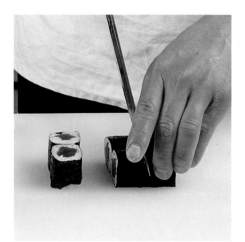

8

Generally allow 6 pieces per roll, so lay the 2 halves next to each other and cut into thirds.

83

Making Thick Sushi Rolls (Futomaki)

1

Cut one nori sheet in half lengthwise and straighten the sides. Lay ½ sheet of nori shiny side down onto the bamboo rolling mat.

2

Moisten your hands with some tezu and get a handful of sushi rice. Spread the rice evenly over the surface of the nori.

3

Add the desired amount of wasabi along the middle of the rice.

4

And also some Japanese mayonnaise.

84

5

Add the fillings you wish to use, placing them in the middle and on top of the wasabi and mayonnaise.

6

Start rolling the mat up over the ingredients, stopping when you get to about 1in/2½cm away from the end of the nori.

7

Lift the mat up and roll forward again to join the edges of the nori together, while at the same time applying a small amount of pressure to make the roll firm.

8

Using a sharp knife, cut the completed rolls in half, place the halves next to each other and cut into thirds. Each roll will provide 6 pieces.

85

Making Inside-Out Rolls (Sakamaki)

1

Cut one nori sheet in half lengthwise and straighten sides. Have ¹/₂ a nori sheet lying on a bamboo rolling mat and pick up a small handful of sushi rice.

2

Spread the rice out evenly over the nori. Once done, take nori and rice off the board and place upsidedown on a damp cloth.

3

Spread the desired amount of wasabi down the centre of the nori.

4

Add ingredients along center of nori.

5

Start rolling the mat up over the ingredients, stopping when you get about 1in/2¹/₂cm away from the end of the nori.

6

Lift the mat up and roll forward again to join the edges of the nori together, while at the same time applying a small amount of pressure to firm the roll.

7

Remove the completed roll from the mat and place onto a plate. Gradually spoon roe around the roll until it coats the rice.

8

Using a sharp knife, cut the completed rolls in half, place the halves next to each other and cut into thirds. Each roll will provide 6 pieces.

Making Temaki-Sushi

1

Start by picking up a half sheet of nori in one hand and a handful of rice about the size of a golf ball in the other.

2

Place rice on one side of the nori sheet and start spreading it out, covering only half of the nori sheet.

3
With your finger or a spoon, rub the desired amount of wasabi along the rice.

4
Add desired fillings to the roll, placing them from one corner down to the middle of the opposite side.

5
Fold the nearest corner of the nori over the filling, and start to shape into a cone.

6
The finished temaki-sushi should be coned-shaped with no rice falling out from the bottom.

89

Making Battleship Sushi (Gunkan Makizushi)

1

Dip your hand in tezu, take a small handful of rice and mould it into a rectangular shape.

2

Wrap fingers from one hand around and over rice. Position thumb from same hand at the end of the rice, bringing the forefinger and middle finger from other hand on top. Gently squeeze to firm it.

3

Cut a nori sheet into strips 1½in/4cm wide. This should give 5–6 pieces per sheet.

4

The hand holding the rice should be wet with tezu, and the other hand that is handling the nori should be dry. Position the piece of rice onto the nori strip.

5

Wrap the nori around the rice, and for holding the ends together, apply a little bit of tezu to make the roll secure.

6

Add the desired amount of wasabi with your finger.

7

Now the topping can be added. Spoon enough in until it reaches the top of the nori.

8

Battleship sushi should be eaten fairly soon after making, since the liquid from the topping may drain through, losing some of the flavor.

Making Sushi Omelet

Instructions

1   Combine dashi, sugar, salt, mirin and soy sauce, stirring until sugar and
     salt have dissolved.

2   Beat in the eggs, being careful not to aerate the mixture if possible.

ingredients:

⅓ cup/75mL/2½fl oz **dashi fish stock
(available from Asian food stores)**

3 tablespoons/45mL **sugar**

1 pinch **salt**

1 tablespoon/15mL **mirin**

2 tablespoons/30mL **light soy sauce**

8 **eggs**

1

Heat up the omelet pan (or ordinary
frying pan), adding a little vegetable oil
with a paper towel. Pour a little omelet
mix into the pan, allowing just a thin
layer to form.

2

Using chopsticks (or a spatula), try to
flatten out any bubbles that may appear.

Making Sushi Omelet

3

When it appears the omelet is almost cooked, or at least firm, tilt the pan up on its side, while at the same time slightly shaking the pan so the omelet becomes loose.

4

Using chopsticks, fold the omelet in half, bringing it from the elevated side closest to you down on top of the other half. Oil the pan again with a paper towel.

5

Add some more mixture to the pan.

6

Lift the cooked omelet and slightly tilt the pan, allowing the mixture to flow underneath. When firm, fold the omelet over as before.

7

Continue to add, cook and fold the omelet until mixture is used up.

8

The end result. Note the layers of the omelet.

Making Tempura Batter

Instructions

Japanese frying techniques are not unlike ours, but because of the close attention to the batter with which the food is often coated, and to the condition and temperature of the oil, Japanese fried foods are especially notable for their delicacy.

Note: The batter should be somewhat thin and watery, and easily run off a spoon. If it is too thick, thin it with drops of cold water. Ideally, the batter should be used shortly after being made, but may be used up to 10 minutes after being made.

ingredients:

1 egg yolk

1 cup/250mL/8fl oz iced water

4 ice cubes

1½ cups/375mL all-purpose flour

1

Add the egg yolk to a large bowl.

Making Tempura Batter

2

Add water and ice cubes into the bowl with the egg.

3

Using chopsticks or a fork, beat the egg yolk and iced water until combined.

4

Sift the flour and add to egg and water mixture.

5

Mix well until ingredients are incorporated.

Filleting Roundfish

Wash fish and leave wet as this makes it easier to scale. Remove scales using a knife or scaler. Start at the tail and scrape towards the head.

Clip the dorsal fin with scissors or, if desired, remove both the dorsal and anal fins by cutting along the side of the fin with a sharp knife. Then pull the fin towards the head to remove it.

For boning or filleting, cut off the head behind gill opening. Use a sharp knife and cut open belly from head to just above anal fin. Remove membranes, veins and viscera. Rinse thoroughly.

To preserve shape of roundfish, cut through the gills, opening outer gill with the thumb. Put a finger into the gill and snag the inner gill. Gently pull to remove inner gill and viscera. Rinse well.

When skinning a whole roundfish, make a slit across the body, behind the gills, with another just above the tail. Then make another cut down the back.

Using a sharp knife, start at the tail and separate the skin from the flesh. Pull the knife towards the head, while holding the skin firmly with the other hand. Do not saw the knife.

Place fillet skin-side down, and cut a small piece of flesh away from the skin close to the tail. Hold skin tight and run a sharp knife along the skin.

Filleting Flatfish

To gut, make a small cut behind gills and pull out viscera.

Skin the whole flatfish by first turning the dark side up and then cutting across the skin where the tail joins the body. With a sharp knife, peel the skin back towards the head until you have enough skin to hold with one hand.

Anchor the fish with one hand and pull the skin over the head. Turn fish over and hold the head while pulling the skin down to the tail.

Place skinned fish on chopping board with eyes up. Cut from head to tail through the flesh in the middle of the fish to the backbone. Insert a sharp knife between the ribs and the end of the fillet near the head. Pull knife down the fillet on one side of the backbone and remove.

Cut off the remaining fillet in the same manner. Turn fish over and remove the two bottom fillets.

Oysters

If you use technique rather than strength, oysters are easy to open. It is best to hold the unopened oyster in a garden glove or tea towel (which will protect your hand from the rough shell) while you open the shell with an oyster knife, held in the other hand.

Hold the oyster with the deep cut down and insert the tip of the oyster knife into the hinge, then twist to open the shell. Do not open oyster by attempting to insert the oyster knife into the front lip of the shell.

Squid and cuttlefish

Rinse in cold water and then cut off tentacles, just above the eye. Squeeze the thick centre part of the tentacles. This will push out the hard beak, which you should discard.

Squeeze the entrails out by running your fingers from the closed to the open end. Pull out the quill and discard.

Peel off skin by slipping finger under it. Pull off the edible fins from either side and also skin them.

Fish Quality Guidelines

The most important thing when making sushi is that the fish is really fresh. Eel and octopus are always cooked. Here are some guidelines on judging the quality and freshness of fish and shellfish:

- A fresh fish should have shiny and almost sparkling skin.
- Its body should be stiff and the meat firm when touched.
- Most fresh fish have clear eyes.
- The tail should not be dried out or curled up at the end.
- It should smell like the ocean (or like a clean pond if it's a freshwater fish).
- It should not smell fishy.
- The scales on a fresh fish should adhere tightly.
- The gills should be cherry-red and should not have any white slime.
- Never buy what seems to be the last pieces of a fillet (try to get a piece of a new one instead).
- Most shellfish should have tightly closed shells.
- Sometimes mussels gape slightly, but they should close quickly when tapped.
- Oysters should always be closed and stored flat so that their liquids don't drain out.
- Try to make the fishmonger your last stop when shopping so you can rush home and put the fish in the refrigerator.
- At home remove whole fish from its wrapping and rinse it off with cold water before putting it in the fridge. If you're not going to use the fish within an hour arrange the fish on ice in a colander over a large bowl. If you store the fish in a bowl with ice you might end up with the fish sitting in a puddle of water, damaging the fish.
- Shellfish, mussels and oysters should be kept in a bowl covered with a wet towel in the refrigerator.

Sushi Bar Survival

Sushi isn't just for lucky people anymore. You can find it anywhere, including pre-packaged at the neighborhood grocery. But the best place to get the full flavor of the experience is still the sushi bar.

At first glance, the restaurant doesn't seem unusual. Some customers sit on floor mats at low tables, while others may choose a more traditional table.

However, if you want to be where the action is, sit at the sushi bar. This is where the sushi chef holds court over a small mountain of seafood, well displayed so you may inspect its freshness, color and texture. Here you will find a myriad of whole fish and shellfish and sheets of seaweed wrapping papers.

The chef — outfitted in a short-sleeved smock and a bright headband — is working non-stop magic with a ball of rice and the prettiest chunk of bright orange salmon you've ever seen.

Every so often a waitress will walk by with a tray for the tables in the back. There are dark green, cone-shaped California rolls, with fish and avocado in them, while other interesting rolls have fresh tuna or cucumber as their center.

As you take a seat your chef or waitress will offer you a menu — usually with full-color photographs and descriptions in English. You'll also be offered something to drink, and you will face your first — and most important — test . . . try the sake!

Sake is a Japanese wine, made from fermented rice, and is traditional with fish dishes. It is potent, fragrant and faintly sweet. But before you begin, a word of warning: an empty cup is considered rude, so your host will keep the bottom wet. Turn the cup upside down when you've had enough.

Your place setting may cause you anxiety, but don't worry. As there are no knives and forks, you either learn chopsticks or resort to fingers. Both are acceptable. Chopsticks can be frustrating for first-timers. Just as you get the hang of clamping onto that rice block, you dip it and the whole piece disintegrates on the way to your mouth.

You'll find a small bottle of soy sauce (shoyu) and a shallow dish for mixing the sauce with a pinch of wasabi (Japanese horseradish). Try this: invert your sushi and dip the fish side in your shoyu mixture. After all, the idea is to complement the flavor of the fish, not the rice.

You will also find a small mound of gari (ginger) in the corner of your platter. These paper-thin slices, pink and pickled, clear out the previous taste sensation and get you ready for the next one. Think of it as a reset button for your taste buds.

Now all you need to decide is what you'll order first. In this wide universe, there's a meal waiting for diners of all persuasions.

Quick tips for surviving a sushi bar

1 Sit at the sushi bar

It's the only way to get the full flavor of the sushi experience...and you can keep a close eye on the chef.

2 Look for sushi sans fish

Vegetarians and others who aren't yet ready for seafood in the raw can try kappamaki, omelet sushi and miso soup.

3 Know what's raw

Lots of sushi styles are cooked, like the ever-popular California roll. But there are some fine distinctions. For instance, ebi (shrimp) is blanched while ama ebi (sweet shrimp) is served raw.

4 Go for full disclosure

If full disclosure makes you more comfortable you might want to stick with the nigiri-sushi style: it's very straightforward — rice block, fish on top. You know exactly what you're getting into.

5 Don't forget the caviar

Lovers of caviar will likely gravitate toward the gunkan-style "battleship" sushi. This is where the truly exotic seafood lives, from the insides of the spiny sea urchin to the eggs of the Japanese flying fish.

Sushi Etiquette

Using Chopsticks

The chopsticks are picked up with the right hand and arranged for comfortable use with the left. Hold the chopsticks slightly towards the thick end. Reverse the tips of the chopsticks before you help yourself to a community dish. When chopsticks are not in use, return them to the right side of your dish.

At the Bar

First, the experienced sushi eater will order assorted sashimi to give the sushi chef a chance to show off his best fish. Always ask the chef what's good. Sashimi is eaten with chopsticks — it is not fingerfood.

When done with the sashimi, ask for a fresh soy sauce dish. Now you're ready for nigiri-sushi, and no wasabi should be placed in the dish, since wasabi is already between the rice and the fish. Nigiri is meant to be eaten with your hands, so don't waste time fumbling with your chopsticks. Lightly dip the end into soy sauce, then place the fish side onto your tongue. Avoid biting the piece in half, just pop the whole thing in. To choose your next selection, the chef will look at your plate to see how well you are doing, rather than looking at you.

When finished, ask the waitress (not the chef) for the bill. Sushi chefs take pride in their job. Be sure to leave a tip!

Bad Manners

Do not ask for knives. This would imply that the food is so tough it can't be properly eaten without them. Do not pass food to another person with chopsticks. This act parallels passing cremated bones of a deceased relative at a Japanese funeral. Do not scrape rice from chopsticks. Do not eat all the rice at once. Rather, return to it after tasting other dishes. Rice when taken must always be eaten. Do not wave your chopsticks around aimlessly over the food, trying to decide what to take next.

Wasabi

Don't use too much wasabi. Wasabi paralyzes your palate and will hide the subtle flavors of raw fish.

The Sushi Chef

The Samurai Tradition

The spirit of sushi is carried on over the centuries by "shokunin" (traditional master sushi chefs).

The Japanese are great believers in learning through apprenticeship. Before you are even allowed to pick up a knife you must work in the kitchen sweeping, doing dishes and other jobs for at least a couple of years. It may take ten years of training to be considered a master and become the head chef.

Tools

A sushi chef's knives are as important to him as a sword is to a samurai. They are made from carbon steel that can be sharpened to literally cut a hair.

A sushi chef has his own set of knives each of which can cost several hundred dollars. He sharpens them before and after use, cleans them after every few strokes, and wraps them up and keeps them in a safe place every night. Contrary to most knives, sushi knives are sharpened on one side only, which makes for a faster, cleaner cut.

Other Types of Sushi

Campbell roll

A Campbell roll contains salmon, asparagus and mayonnaise. Use the smallest asparagus spears you can find, or cut larger ones into smaller strips. Cut the salmon into long strips about ¹/₂in/1cm wide by ¹/₈in/¹/₂cm thick. The packages of smoked salmon you see in the deli sections of supermarkets are perfect for this. Spread some Japanese mayonnaise along the edge of the roll. Place the salmon on top of this, then top with an equal amount of asparagus.

Virginia roll

A Virginia roll contains crab, eel and mushrooms. Virginians prefer to use real crabmeat, but imitation will work just fine.

Add the crab and eel, like the California, with the eel replacing the avocado. Mushrooms are then placed like the cucumber.

Saikuzushi

Saikuzushi, or festival sushi, is an art form. Rice is tinted different colors, sectioned off and rolled. When it is sliced, complex images are created.

Chakinzushi

Chakinzushi is sushi rice in a thin omelet wrapper shaped and tied like a drawstring purse. Sometimes a single pea or small shrimp decorates the ruffled part of the wrapper.

Fukusazushi

Fukusazushi is a variation of maki-sushi, where a square-molded rice mixture is wrapped in a thin sheet of omelet. This is turned over to conceal the seams and garnished with a nori ribbon and ginger.

Temarizushi

Temarizushi are rice balls tightly wrapped in thinly sliced marinated fish.

Favorites

If there is one word to describe Japanese cuisine, it is "artistic." It is a cuisine in harmony with nature, according food awesome respect, and preparing it with an eye for detail. We have included some of the more well-known examples of Japanese foods. Try them as a follow up to some sushi and sashimi...

Prawn Tempura

ingredients:

6 large green prawns
1 recipe tempura batter (see page 94)
flour for coating prawns
vegetable cooking oil

Tempura Sauce

Combine soy sauce, dashi (fish stock) and mirin in equal quantities and boil for 20 minutes over low heat. Allow to cool. Best if served chilled.

Serves 2

Instructions

1   Shell and de-vein prawns, then cut 4 incisions into the under-sections to straighten them out.

2   Prepare tempura batter (see page 94).

3   Dip each prawn in flour and then in batter (twirl it around to properly coat it), then drop into hot oil (400°F/200°C).
    Only fry 5 pieces of food at a time.

4   Fry until golden brown. Remove and drain, serve with tempura sauce and grated horseradish or lemon.

Note: Keep oil clean during cooking by using a slotted spoon to remove food particles from oil as they appear.

This recipe by no means encompasses all of the ingredients that may be used in tempura.

Substitutions and additions might include:

Slices of fish fillets $1/4$in/$1/2$mm thick, slices of carrot $1/4$in/$1/2$mm thick, skewered sections of green onion, small asparagus stalks, slices of sweet potato $1/4$in/$1/2$mm thick, and many other ingredients from beans to snow peas and eggplant.

Japanese Breakfast

The traditional Japanese breakfast consists of a bowl of hot boiled short grain rice mixed with raw egg, nori flakes and soy sauce.

This is a very simple meal, and should be arranged with side dishes such as Japanese pickles, tofu and miso soup (miso-shuru). To the majority of Japanese, breakfast is not breakfast without this savory, aromatic soup.

Miso soup ingredients:

250g/8oz **tofu**

½ cup/125mL/4fl oz **miso paste**

½ cup/125mL/4fl oz **dashi stock**

1 tablespoon/15mL **mirin**

1 **green onion, chopped**

4 cups/1 litre **water**

Instructions

1   Boil water with the dashi.

2   Mix the miso and mirin together and add to the boiling liquid.

3   Dice the tofu into cubes and place into the hot stock and heat on medium for 5 minutes.

4   Serve in small individual dishes sprinkled with chopped green onions.

Serves 4–5

Sukiyaki

ingredients

3oz /100g Japanese cabbage

4 green onions

2 bamboo shoots (Takenoko)

20oz /600g rib eye beef

1 carrot

4oz/125g tofu

3oz /100g Japanese mushrooms (shiitake)

4 spinach leaves

2 baby corn (or bracken, carrots, daikon, etc.)

1 portion warishita (see below)

2oz/60g piece of suet

3oz /100g rice noodles (vermicelli)

3 raw eggs

warishita (sukiyaki sauce)

1 cup/240mL/8fl oz soy sauce

1/4 cup/50mL/2fl oz mirin

1/2 cup/125mL sugar

pinch salt

1 cup/240mL/8fl oz chicken stock or dashi

1 Slice the Japanese cabbage into 2in/5cm slices. Cut the green onions into 3in/7½cm lengths and thinly slice the bamboo shoots and beef. Cut the carrot into fine shreds and cut the tofu into small squares. Soak mushrooms in warm water for 10 minutes. Soak the vermicelli in a bowl of warm water for 30 minutes until tender. Roll the spinach leaves up and cut as green onions. Cut the baby corn cobs in half.

2 To make the warishita (sukiyaki sauce) combine the soy sauce, mirin, sugar, salt and stock in a saucepan and heat for 30 minutes on low heat.

3 Heat a large frying pan and place the suet in it. Use this to grease the base of the pan. Gently fry the beef pieces and the green onions. When tender, pour over some of the warishita sauce then add remaining ingredients (except the eggs) to the pan and continue to cook gently until tender. Repeat until all the sauce is used.

4 During the frying process add some sake or water to the pan to prevent excessive flavor development of the warishita and to maintain a balance of flavors throughout the cooking.

5 To serve sukiyaki, place the beaten egg in a bowl and use for dipping the sukiyaki pieces into. The raw egg is optional and not always used by western people. Sukiyaki can be served from the pot into small bowls of rice.

Serves 4

Yakitori

ingredients:
yakitori sauce
3 tablespoons/45mL sake
1/2 cup/125mL/4fl oz soy sauce
1/2 cup/125mL/4oz sugar
pinch of salt
dash kombu (kelp stock)

3 1/2oz /100g chicken breasts, cut into 2in/5cm pieces
1 green onion, cut into 2in/5cm pieces
4 bamboo skewers

Instructions

1   Combine all yakitori sauce ingredients and cook 30 minutes
    on low heat.

2   Thread prepared chicken and green onions onto skewers.
    Grill over a high heat or coals, turning occasionally until
    the juices begin to flow.

3   Brush with yakitori sauce or dip into the sauce and continue
    grilling until cooked to your liking.

Note: In Japan a lot of chicken and meat parts are substituted as
desired, such as giblet, liver, heart, etc.

Serves 1

Teriyaki Chicken

ingredients:

3 teaspoons/15mL sugar

¼ cup/60mL/2fl oz sake

¼ cup/60mL/2fl oz mirin

½ cup/125mL/4fl oz light soy sauce

4 chicken thighs

Teriyaki can be applied to a wide variety of meats and seafood. Teriyaki fish cutlets, prawns, beef and squid are just a few. These can be barbecued or grilled using this versatile marinade.

Instructions

1   To make marinade, combine sugar, sake, mirin and soy sauce.

2   Bone the chicken thighs, leaving skin intact.

3   Place chicken into a dish, add about half the teriyaki marinade and marinate for 6–8 hours.

4   Remove chicken from marinade and place on barbecue about 8in/20cm from moderate coals.

5   Cook for about 45 minutes, or until cooked.

6   Add remaining marinade to a saucepan and reduce to about half. Serve with the cooked chicken.

Serves 4

Stuffed Fried Bean Curd Bags

ingredients:

10 pieces thin deep-fried tofu (aburage)

$^2/_3$ cup/165mL/5$^1/_2$fl oz dashi broth

3 tablespoons/45mL soy sauce

2 tablespoons/25mL sugar

1 tablespoon/15mL sake

1 $^1/_2$ cups/375mL sushi rice

1 tablespoon/15mL toasted sesame seeds

$^1/_4$ grated boiled carrot

Instructions

1   Cut aburage into halves and pull open the center of the pieces, making bags. (Like preparing pita bread).

2   In a saucepan, combine dashi broth, soy sauce, sugar and sake. Bring to the boil and simmer the bean curd bags for 10–15 minutes. Remove from heat, drain and cool.

3   Mix the sushi rice with sesame seeds and carrot.

4   Fill the bags with the rice mixture and roll the top of the bean curd over the rice to enclose it. Be careful not to add too much rice or the bags will split.

Makunouchi

ingredients:

1 cooked bamboo shoot

1 cooked mushroom

I piece of cooked bean curd

2 prawns

1 piece of grilled yellowtail or garfish

1 cooked king prawn

1 combination sashimi

1 nagashimono (Japanese sweet jelly)

1 makunouchi box

7 pieces makunouchi rice

The Makunouchi bentoo emerged in the Edo Period in Edo (now Tokyo) as the meal of choice during intermission at the kabuki theater (the word "makunouchi" means the interval between acts). Makunouchi is now a standard type of obentoo available at train stations and bentoo shops. The sushi rice is shaped into little cylinders and sprinkled with sesame seeds.

Instructions

The ingredients are presented in a decorative lacquer box in combinations carefully arranged for artistic effect.

Makunouchi Nigiri

ingredients:

1 ½ cups/375mL sushi rice

I teaspoon/5mL roasted sesame seeds

1 sheet nori, for nori belts

steamed asparagus

sliced cucumber

assorted fish fillet

cuttlefish

Instructions

1   Make 8–10 pieces Makunouchi rice by rolling rice into bite-sized pieces and sprinkling with toasted sesame seeds.

2   Place each of the ingredients in sushi-cut style on top of rice.

3   Wrap nori belt around the pieces that require it (see page 29).

Note: Use any combination of ingredients that is available.

Glossary

Anago (sea or conger eel)

Anago is a leaner version of unagi (freshwater eel). It is always boiled first, then grilled. Because it is served with a special mixture made from sugar, soy sauce and eel stock, no dipping sauce or wasabi is needed.

Buzuguri

Chunk-style octopus.

California Roll

Popular for beginning sushi eaters, California rolls are hand rolls of cooked crabmeat, avocado and cucumber.

Ebi (boiled shrimp)

Very popular on sushi menus for their sweet, fresh taste, ebi are shrimp that are boiled in salted water, then shelled and spread into a butterfly shape leaving only the shell of the tails attached. They are usually eaten with wasabi and soy sauce.

Gari (sliced ginger)

A garnish used to freshen the palate between sushi plates, gari is fresh ginger that has been pickled in salt and sweet vinegar. For best results when buying gari for making sushi, select firm knobs with smooth skin.

Gunkan

Known as "battleship" sushi, gunkan is a type of nigiri-sushi that is made by wrapping a band of seaweed around a pad of rice that is pressed down so ingredients can lay on top. This is an easy way to serve fish roe and other smaller ingredients.

Hamachi (yellowtail)

Hamachi is a variety of yellowtail. It is light yellow in color and has a rich, smooth, smoky taste. Sushi chefs consider the tail and the cheek of the fish the best part and this is often saved and cooked for special customers.

Hiro Special

This sushi is wrapped reverse style, with the rice on the outside, and it contains cream cheese, cucumber, crab, avocado, salmon and tuna.

Ikura (salmon roe)

These are the red, shiny, ball-like fish eggs. The name ikura derives from "ikra," a Russian word for fish roe or caviar. This is why ikura is sometimes used as red caviar as well as a delicious sushi dish.

Glossary

Kani (crab)

Always served cooked, kani is an excellent choice for sushi beginners. It can be enjoyed as nigiri-sushi or wrapped in seaweed as it is served in California rolls. Kani is realcrab meat, while kanikama is artificial crabmeat, used sometimes for certain types of sushi.

Kyuri

Cucumber wrapped with seaweed.

Maguro (tuna)

Maguro is the most popular item sold at sushi bars due to its familiarity and fresh, clean taste. Though there are many varieties of tuna, yellowfin (ahi) or bluefin lean cut tuna is what is used for sushi. Buy yellowfin in winter and early spring when it's at its peak and bluefin is out of season.

Maki-sushi or maki sushi (rolled sushi)

A type of sushi made by wrapping rice, fish and other ingredients into a long seaweed roll, then slicing it into bite-sized pieces.

There are two types of maki-sushi rolls: hosomaki, a slender roll made into 6 small pieces and temaki, a hand roll which is eaten in 2–3 bites and resembles the shape of an ice cream cone. Maki-sushi is served with soy sauce and pickled ginger.

Makisu

Used for preparing rolled sushi, a makisu is a mat made from bamboo sticks tied together with cotton string. If you're going to make rolled sushi, this is an essential tool.

Masago (smelt roe)

Masago are small orange flying fish eggs, a prized delicacy in Japan. Masago can be prepared as nigiri-sushi, gunkan or maki-sushi and is often used for garnishing the outside of hand rolls. It is closely related to tobiko, a flying fish roe; though slightly lighter in color, masago shares its taste and texture: salty and resistant to the bite.

Nigiri-sushi or nigiri-zushi

Meaning "pressed by the hand," nigiri-sushi is a slice of cooked or uncooked fish pressed across a pad of rice. Fish roe is also made into nigiri-sushi, in which case a strip of seaweed is wrapped around it to hold it together. Nigiri-sushi is often served with wasabi and is meant to be dipped in soy sauce.

Sake (salmon)

Salmon is a very popular kind of sushi, easily recognizable by its bright orange color and sweet, tender flavor. Salmon is never served raw in sushi bars; rather, it is lightly smoked first or it is cured in salt and sugar for a few days and then served.

Sashimi

Sashimi means "raw fish." It is eaten with no rice, though it is often dipped in soy sauce and eaten with wasabi and ginger. Sashimi is carefully selected from the purest waters and is prepared by specially trained sashimi chefs to ensure the highest quality fish. Sashimi is generally eaten at the beginning of the meal before the sushi.

Sonosan Roll

Cheese, cucumber, avocado and tuna.

Sushi

Japanese staple that combines vinegar-flavored rice with fish. Sushi comes in many forms and can be eaten with chopsticks or with your hands. The most common types of sushi are nigiri-sushi (hand made sushi), and maki-sushi (rolled sushi made with a bamboo mat). Additionally, sashimi is raw fish that is very commonly eaten along with a sushi meal.

Suzuki (sea bass)

Japanese fish with shiny white flesh and mild flavour. Sometimes it is served as sashimi that is called "suzuki usu zukuri."

Tako (octopus)

Tako is recognizable by its burgundy tentacles; in fact, the legs of the octopus are actually more commonly eaten than the body. Tako is always boiled to tenderize the flesh and leave the meat with a slightly chewy and subtle flavour.

Tekka Maki

A raw tuna and rice roll. The name "tekka" refers to the gambling parlors in Japan, where this snack was served at the gaming table as finger-food.

Unagi (freshwater eel)

Unagi is similar to anago (sea eel) in color and taste. Instead of being boiled first, however, it is grilled, then glazed with a mixture of soy sauce, suga, and eel broth. The sauce makes the flavor sweet and rich, and it should be eaten without any dipping sauce.

Uni (sea urchin)

For the brave sushi eater, uni is considered a delicacy in many parts of the world. What is actually served is the gonads of the sea urchin. Its soft texture, held in place with a band of nori, has a delicious, subtle, nut-like flavor and is a definite favorite among advanced sushi eaters.

Wasabi (horseradish)

A spicy green horseradish paste with a very pungent taste that helps to bring out the flavor of sushi.

Sushi à la Carte

aburage — deep-fried tofu pouches

aji — horse mackerel

akagai — ark shell or pepitoma clam

ama-ebi — raw shrimp

anago — sea or conger eel

aoyagi — round clam

awabi — abalone

ayu— sweetfish

buri — adult yellowtail

chutoro — marbled tuna belly

ebi — boiled shrimp

hamachi — young yellowtail

hamaguri — clam

hamo — pike conger; sea eel

hatahata — sandfish

hikari-mono — various kinds of "shiny" fish, such as mackerel

himo — "fringe" around an ark shell

hirame — flounder or halibut

hokkigai — surf clam

hotategai — scallop

ika — squid

ikura — salmon roe

inada — very young yellowtail

kaibashira — eye of scallop or shellfish valve muscles

kaiware — daikon radish sprouts

kajiki — swordfish

kani — crab

kanpachi — lean yellowtail

karei — sole or flatfish

katsuo — bonito tuna

kazunoko — herring roe

kohada — gizzard shad

kuruma-ebi — prawn

maguro — tuna

makajiki — blue marlin

masu — trout

meji (maguro) — young tuna

mekajiki — swordfish

mirugai — surf, geoduck or horseneck clam

negi-toro — tuna belly and chopped green onion

ni-ika — squid simmered in a soy-flavored stock

nori-tama — sweetened egg wrapped in dried seaweed

otoro — fatty portion of tuna belly

saba — mackerel

sake — salmon

sawara — Spanish mackerel

sayori — (springtime) halfbeak

seigo — young sea bass

shako — mantis shrimp

shima-aji — yellow jack

shime-saba — mackerel (marinated)

shiromi — seasonal "white meat" fish

suzuki — sea bass

tai — red snapper

tairagai — razor-shell clam

tako — cooked octopus

tamago — sweet egg custard wrapped in dried seaweed

torigai — Japanese cockle

toro — fatty tuna belly

tsubugai — Japanese shellfish

uni — sea urchin roe

Maki-sushi (sushi rolls)

ana-kyu-maki — conger eel and cucumber rolls

chutoro-maki — marbled tuna roll

futo-maki — a thick roll filled with rice, omelet, avocado and bits of vegetables

kaiware-maki — daikon sprout roll

kanpyo-maki — pickled gourd rolls

kappa-maki — cucumber-filled maki-sushi

maguro-temaki — tuna temaki

maki-mono — vinegared rice and fish (or other ingredients) rolled in nori seaweed

natto-maki — sticky, strong-tasting fermented soybean rolls

negitoro-maki — tuna and green onion roll

nori-maki — same as kanpyo maki; in Osaka, same as futo-maki

oshinko-maki — pickled daikon (radish) rolls

otoro-maki — fatty tuna roll

tekka-maki — tuna-filled maki-sushi

tekkappa-maki — selection of both tuna and cucumber rolls

temaki — hand-rolled cones

umejiso-maki — Japanese ume plum and perilla-leaf roll

Other sushi terms

battera-zushi — oshi-zushi topped with mackerel

chakin-zushi — vinegared rice wrapped in a thin egg crepe

chirashi-zushi — assorted raw fish and vegetables over rice

Edomae-zushi — same as nigiri-zushi

gari — vinegared ginger

inari-zushi — vinegared rice and vegetables wrapped in fried tofu pouches

neta — sushi topping

nigiri-sushi or nigiri-zushi — pieces of raw fish over vinegared rice **odori-ebi** — live ("dancing") shrimp

oshinko — Japanese pickles

oshi-zushi — Osaka-style sushi: squares of pressed rice topped with vinegared/cooked fish

sashimi — raw fish (without rice)

shoyu — soy sauce

tataki — pounded, almost raw fish

tekka-don — pieces of raw tuna over rice

wasabi — Japanese horseradish

Index

Notes

Notes